The Bulletproof Breakup Guide for Men

How to Get Over a Breakup, Heal a Broken Heart, and Move On

Marcus Manual

Table of Contents

Introduction

It felt like being hit by a shotgun fired at a 5-meter distance straight to the heart. I thought that it would be painful, but for the first few days, I could not feel anything. Maybe it was a blessing not to feel, but it was an immobilizing kind of numbness, the kind that had me staring in space blankly for hours. The bullet had been well crafted and the aim was sure. There was no gunfire, no warning shots, and no resounding noise. She shot me in the heart and out of consciousness when she uttered quietly but firmly, the words, "I'm sorry, it's over."

Janine had been my life. From the first moment I saw her, I knew I wanted to see her for the rest of my life. We were officemates back then, with our cubicles facing each other's back. I was the new guy then at the office and she had been with the group for some years back. I had been office-hopping for some time and I thought that the next one would just be another 6 months hiccup before the next. But when I laid my eyes on her, I was convinced I wanted to sit in that desk beside her forever. Perhaps it was her eyes that caught me, her sparkling blue eyes that would smile from the corners. She wasn't the laughing kind, but it was her eyes that sparked all the joy from her. Or perhaps it was that gentle touch when she nudged me over to my seat, that instant spark of connection when her hand touched my back, running electricity all over my body. Or perhaps it was her low-set voice, calming and reassuring but also sexy music to my ears. Or perhaps it was everything about her that made me feel I loved her at first sight.

We started dating quite immediately. I asked her out after the second week of work. It was just a simple dinner and a bowling night – not the most original nor the most romantic of dinners. But the conversation just flowed through us. During the appetizer, she opened up about office politics and how she hadn't been promoted for a long time. Soup time came and we were talking about childhood memories. The main course opened the way for exes and past relationships. By the time we were at our second wine glass, our hands were exploring. We didn't even reach the bowling alley because she stayed the night over. From there, it was just one beautiful day after the other. We were happy, having found our lost better half.

It wasn't the most perfect of relationships. I loved her to bits and I felt she loved me. But we would fight at times over the pettiest of things. She didn't like my messiness in the room or my procrastination. I would fret over her obsessive compulsion and her nagging. She would get mad when I didn't flush the toilet in the morning, leaving spills everywhere. I would complain when she threw out old things that had sentimental value for me. We were a normal couple who fought. But on most days, we got along well.

I loved her so much that in spite and because of everything we went through, I actually proposed to her one November night. I set up everything to be perfect for the occasion. I colluded with her friends to fake invite her to go somewhere shopping. I hired a professional chef and set up a romantic dinner in her pad. I even flooded her unit with pink carnations, her favorite. I dressed my best to impress, holding the 10k ring I had saved up 6 months' worth of salary for. She was worth all the hard work, the toxicity in the office, the sleepless nights. When finally, she opened the door, I was beaming in excitement. But what would have been the most romantic nights of my life became the most traumatic. When Janine opened that door, she wasn't alone. She entered holding the hands of one of the guys at work I barely knew. I didn't know if I should drop to my knees and say the lines I practiced a couple of times over and over or I should just punch the guy outright. I didn't know what to do so I just froze on the stop. And then she came over and shot me her lines, "I'm sorry, it's over."

I tried winning her back in the next couple of weeks. My ego was hurt, but I loved her more than myself. I ate my ego up and called her many times. She kept on repeating over and over that she just got tired of us, of me. I couldn't understand how she could do this to me. I thought we were doing ok, fighting yes, but still communicating. Janine said she was tired of our relationship that was going nowhere. She couldn't see herself marrying me. I tried to press her that I would change, that I would try to make amends. But she said, she already found someone who was fit for her. Whenever I would call her up and get rejected, I would die from the multiple shots she fired.

It was a difficult journey for me. It was the darkest of times when I felt so alone, so betrayed, so devastated. Janine had been my life and without her, I felt nothing. I even felt worthless. I went through a phase of isolating myself from friends, withdrawing from work, spending the morning drunk at random bars, getting into random fights and sleeping a lot. There was a point where I even thought about ending my own life. But what saved me was writing. In my sadness, I turned to my old passion which was writing. I would write away all my feelings and thoughts, my hate for Janine, my love for Janine. Writing saved me. And this book is a testament to that dark journey. This book was made in pain and filled with a lot of tears. But this book also helped me become stronger. This is your bulletproof vest you can carry as you travel through the pains of breakups. If you are out there in the dark, I can feel you. Let this book help you through the darkest nights of a breakup.

Chapter 1: What NOT to Do in the Immediate Aftermath

So, you are hurt and angry. You were left out, which is quite unusual for you. This may be your first time to be rejected, which is the most painful. Or you may have been rejected a couple of times already, yet each new one is more painful than the first. It might be hard to imagine that men have breakup issues or that they are on the losing side of breakups in the first place. But it happens. It happened to me, maybe it is happening to you, and it is actually happening more times than you imagine. Whatever your circumstance may be, you are here reading this book. Before you make any stupid decisions, you are going to regret, let me tell you first what you shouldn't do. Your mind right now is perplexed and disoriented. As such, your feelings might get the better of you and lead you to act in ways that are destructive to yourself, to your ex, and to the people around you. The negative repercussions might even extend for years. Before you make the mistake of your life, be advised on what you shouldn't do. These may constitute the ten commandments of what not to do in a breakup.

DON'T Stalk Your Ex

Yes, you love her so much and you want to win her back. Yes, you might be angry and just curious how she can go on with her life without you. Yes, you can't imagine your life without her. But give each other the space you both need. The other person might need some time to process her feelings and be clarified with how she really feels about you and the situation. You may also need some time for yourself and reassess your relationship. This breakup may even be a blessing because you can have some time to think about your personal lives. So respect that sacred time. Perhaps both of you needed some space just be apart and evaluate your life goals.

We say that this is an immediate move because the more you stalk your ex on her social media pages, the more intense your feelings will become. You are in a confused state right now, and the more expose you are to that person, the more confused you will be. If you are feeling angry, you will feel more anger when you see her posting online. If you are depressed, you will be more depressed when you look at her pictures. If you are hurt, you will be in more pain when you see her going out with others. Refrain from going to her house, following her on the road, waiting for her in corners. You are not loving her if you are stalking her. That is called obsession and that may lead you to act in ways that might harm the both of you and your future relationships. Repress that urge and turn your attention and pain somewhere else.

DON'T Drink Yourself to Death

It is normal for people to drown their sorrows with alcohol. The bar is the best place to hear breakup stories as people loosen up due to the effect of alcohol. Strangers become quick friends in a bar of sorrows. You might see this much in movies, but in reality, binge drinking is not a pretty sight. Alcohol may help you open up and release your sorrows, but it may actually hurt you in the long run.

One, when you binge drink, you don't control how much you spend. Bottles may just come and go for the drunk, and you claim that you deserve to be drunk. Before you know it, your tab might be piling up expenses way beyond your budget. Alcohol may even make you more gregarious than usual. In your drunkenness, other people may even take advantage of you, and you end up spending for drinks and food you didn't even consume. A drunk man is the most generous friend you can have.

Second, drunkenness may release your inhibition that will lead you to make decisions you would regret. We've all heard about drunk calls where you ring up your ex in your drunkenness and say things you shouldn't be saying. Drunk people also do the most stupid of things. They can dance naked on a table top, pick-up fights with random strangers, and vomit all over the place, destroy property and say the loudest, funniest and most embarrassing of statements. We live in a social media age right now, and one click of your drunkenness episode would be online forever, your shame displayed for eternity.

Third, you can carry over this behavior which may affect your mental health. Substance abuse disorders are diagnosed frequently in people who may have been undergoing a lot of stress in their lives such as a breakup. Their turning to alcohol may become a disorder, both affecting their mental and physical health. From one bottle, you can graduate easily to a whole case, to more cases of beer. Your alcohol may spread to illegal drugs to higher doses which may kill you. Alcohol is addicting and may be difficult to shake off. From one problem of a breakup, you may be faced with more problems.

DON'T Hook Up with Random People

So, you are drunk in a bar, you came for a breakup and you are in a lot of pain. The worst possible thing you can do is to start another relationship with another person you just met. The alcohol may have loosened your inhibition, so you became bolder and more forward. But you are not exactly in the best position or state to start anything new. It would be terribly unfair of you and for the new girl if you immediately launch any form of sexual or even romantic relationship. You may be suffering now, but your loss may also cause pain on the other person who might also be needing affection. Rebound romances rarely work because people are not in the right frame of mind when they enter into it. After your drunkenness episode, you might not even like the girl you hooked up with. Unless it is clear that it is a one-time affair, hooking up may not be the immediate solution to your pain.

How long will it take before you can hook up with someone? There are some who say that you should observe the 6-month rule. Only after this period could you begin dating other people. But this is just a convention people would like to follow. There are no hard and fast rules, but 6 months may provide you with enough time to resolve your issues with your ex, have a proper state of mind and to be ready to meet someone new. In this way, you are also taking care of the next person you might be interested in. If you mix the timelines between your ex and your present, where they may possibly overlap, then you may face a lot of issues. To make it clean, just stay away from hook-ups immediately after the breakup.

DON'T Carry the Personal Pain to Work

People make the mistake of bringing their personal problems to the workplace. You broke up with your girlfriend of ten years and you feel devastated. And now you think everyone should cooperate with your sadness. This may lead you to do poorly at work. In your sorrow or even drunkenness, you might start being late reporting for work. Your mind may be somewhere else and the output of your presentations may reflect that lack of focus. Yes, people will try to understand. But the company did not breakup with your girl and shouldn't be made to suffer because of your loss. If you don't watch it, people may just be fed up with and this may lead to bigger problems, the worst of which is to be fired from work.

It is good to distinguish between your personal and your work life, however hard that may be. In my case, it was really difficult because she was also my workmate. It even came to the point where she left the office just so we could be apart. The negativity in one aspect of your life shouldn't affect the other aspects, however painful that might be. It will also help you to move on if you simply focus on the work and not on your personal problems. In this way, you are channeling your pain into something productive. Use your hurt and excel at work so something good may come out of something negative.

DON'T Make Any Major Financial Move

The same principle as the above advice apply here. You are again very much unstable and prone to reckless decisions. In your desire to fill up the space vacated inside you, there might be a strong urge to spend. This can range to a therapeutic shopping to outright dangerous spree. Perhaps you think you need that new camera to help you cope. Or you might feel you deserve that brand new Porsche. Or just to spite everyone, you might want to sell out your hard-earned flat. Don't. Before you can even think about touching your savings after a breakup, think about how hard it would be for you to regain that money. In your lucid moments, think if you really have to buy those items or that urge is coming from your hurt. Be honest at how you feel and don't let your feelings get the best out of you.

It might be good if you have someone you trust and is not involved in your relationship to talk you out of major financial decisions. It can be a friend or a family member who has seen how much you have worked hard. It is easier to spend your money than to actually earn it, so you would need the best advice to take care of your hard-earned money. You might think that your beloved is more important than any money in the world. That might be true, but it isn't worth wasting all your savings on buying items you and your ex-girlfriend may not use at all. Temper your urge and keep your wallet away from you.

DON'T Rush to Be Happy

When people ask you, "Are you ok?", it is alright to say that you are not. When people try to comfort you, don't brush them away and say that you are fine. When people reach out to you, stop the urge to force a smile or to crack a joke. It is ok not to be ok. And people should recognize that from you. They will understand that this is a difficult time for you and so you don't need to put up a front that you are in top shape. It will really seem highly artificial if you are all smiles the next day after your breakup and greeting everyone in the office. It might even come across to others that you are taking the situation very lightly and that you might not have been serious in the first place.

Pain will take time. It does not happen in a minute or the hour that you broke up. It might even take months or years before you can even say that you are ok. And it is totally ok if you take your time with your pain. Don't compare yourself with others who might be over the girl in a few weeks or in some in a few decades. The more you compare, the more pressure you will feel. Focus on your own process and be gentle with yourself.

DON'T Take Your Own Life

It is in the most depressing of times when you will feel most worthless, most hopeless. Your breakup might affect all aspects of your life. It may lead you to not perform well in the office. It might lead you to cut off ties from others. It will also poison your mind with thoughts that keep on running over and over your head. The breakup may induce you to think negatively about yourself. You might start questioning your talents, your capacities, your accomplishments. You might think negatively about the world. You may develop trust issues and be jaded about your opinions on relationships. You might think about how hopeless the future will be, that there is nothing good that is going to happen in the world.

These will slowly poison your mind and you might enter thoughts of ending your life just to escape the pain. Don't. You are far too good to die. There are better ways to get back at the girl than taking your own life. What you are undergoing might be the most painful you have experienced. But that doesn't mean that you can take your own life. The pain will eventually pass away. If you kill yourself, then you will not be able to experience life after that pain. Undergo the hurt and triumph over it at the other end. If you become consumed by your pain, then you have let sadness and negativity win over you. If you truly love the other person, you also have to love yourself.

These are just some important reminders for you especially when you are fresh from the breakup. That special time after the official breakup is especially hurtful for you, exposing your vulnerabilities. The pain will consume you physically, mentally and emotionally. So, anticipate these and follow the commandments so you don't do anything you will regret later on in your life. You are going to look back at this moment someday and think how dramatic the breakup was or how petty the commotion was. You will revisit your behavior and thoughts and you might even find it funny how you reacted at that time. So, remember these guidelines and tread courageously along that path of hurt and redemption.

Chapter 2: Your Body During a Breakup

At this point, you might observe some changes happening to your body when you break up. It is important to take note of these physical changes because they will reinforce the mental and emotional processes you may be undergoing. Conversely, what you may be feeling right now will have an impact on your body. When you begin to understand the body in pain, you will be able to anticipate the changes and prepare better for this. Breakups are painful but you still have to maintain your physical health in order to support your emotional and mental pain. Other people will be the ones who will actually notice the physical differences first because you might be preoccupied mentally with your pain. A friend may point out that you seem spaced out and lost in thought. A family member may notice that you have lost weight over the past weeks. An officemate may give you feedback about your eating habits and the eye bags hanging from loss of sleep. When others recognize these signs, be alert already because the physical differences will affect your mental and emotional well-being.

The very first symptoms that you will notice is a depressed mood. You will feel very gloomy most of the time, even without apparent reason. It might be sunny outside, but you may feel that the weather is quite gloomy. This is a depressed mood that does not easily go away. You might try losing it when you eat food or when you do some exciting. But the depressed mood will stick and linger on. Just allow it to happen because the experience is still fresh. But it will eventually ebb away on its own, even without you doing something artificially to ward it off. Others will notice this sadness as a glum expression on your face. Your eyes may be red from all the crying. You might stare blankly in space. These are all part of the process that a breakup will do to your body.

Another symptom has to do with a diminished pleasure in the usual activities of the day. If ordinarily, your routine work may give you pleasure, when you break up, it might not be as enjoyable as before. You can find eating at a particular restaurant a very romantic experience. But now, you can only remember your ex and your memories together, thus the pleasure is diminished. You may find being promoted something exciting or exhilarating. After a breakup, hearing a promotion might not be as satisfying as before. The depressed mood may be so pervasive that everything is not as pleasurable as before.

Watch out for this because this can lead you to explore risky behaviors in pursuit of pleasure. This may pave the way for substance abuse. You may start out with alcohol. One bottle may have satisfied you. But because of the breakup, one bottle might not be enough. You may soon graduate to two, to three, to four. Before you know, you are consuming cases of beer already just to get your usual dose. And without the high amount of the substance, you may begin to show symptoms of withdrawal. Your body will now be craving that substance or it won't function at all. From alcohol, you may try out illegal drugs, which can also be addicting and eventually destructive. From small consumption, you can easily graduate to heavy and repeated consumption. You might not be able to control later on the addictive hold of alcohol and drugs on you and this might become a medical condition.

Weight is also a factor we have to note. This may either be a significant loss or gain. Weight is affected by how much we eat and how much activity we have. When we break up, we are more prone to either eat so much in order to fill up that emptiness inside or we don't eat at all, as though we have lost the pleasure when we eat. People either become anorexic or obese months after a breakup. When we factor for activity, the effect is more dramatically seen. When people break up, they might feel so sluggish to move or they may busy themselves with more activities just to feel high. Again, the principle of extremities are operating in breakups. These fluctuations in weight as a product of eating and activity extremities are not good for the physical body because they can predispose you to various diseases. Common diseases that result from breakups include peripheral vascular disease, stroke, electrolyte deficiencies and nutritional imbalances. Be conscious of your weight if you go through a breakup.

Check also for the level energy at the end of the day. It might be the case that you really didn't do much at all during a day and yet you feel so tired. Or you might have done the usual activities such as going to the office or having lunch out. But you still feel extra tired as though you did a lot of strenuous things. You may not have done many things physically, but your mind has been racing back and forth with different thoughts. That contributes to your fatigue. When the body is stressed, it will release hormones such as norepinephrine and adrenaline that will prime the body to go on fight or flight mode. This is good when you have an impending danger coming. But when prolonged, this can damage organs and blood vessels. Fatigue is a sign that your body has been exposed to these stress hormones for a prolonged and unnecessary period of time. Watch out if you feel tired unnecessarily because this might be a danger sign already.

There is also a diminished capacity to think or concentrate when you just had a breakup. You might be physically in the office, but your mind is wandering somewhere else. You could be typing the whole hour in the computer but when you check, you are not actually writing anything substantial. You may keep on making mistakes because you are remembering the hurt moment and that can lead to poor work performance. Check yourself if you have started to become more careless at work, if you find it difficult to listen to other people, if you are not able to perform as efficiently as before. The more intense your feelings when you broke up, the more distracted you will be during your activities in other parts of your life.

Sleep is also an important indicator. Again, we want to watch out for extremities in sleep, either too much or too little of it. You can have too much sleep when you feel you just want to forget the whole affair, or you don't want to engage in social interactions. But even with more sleep, you still feel tired. You may also want to have less sleep because you devote most of your waking hours thinking about her. Both of these extremities are bad for your physical health. They can promote different diseases and also lead to poorer appetite and concentration. Sleep affords repair and rest for your organs. Without the good quality of sleep, you simply feel tired and this is bad for your organs. Sleep also consolidates learning. Your brain is able to function better when it has rested. Lack or excess of bad quality of sleep then will lead to poorer memory retention and overall brain function.

These are just some of the symptoms of a breakup. More specifically, these are warning signs of an impending depressive episode which accompanies a traumatic event. You have to observe this on yourself or have someone mirror your behavior to yourself. Persistence of these symptoms over a 6-month period or more already warrants a consultation at a psychiatrist. Your body may have physically changed because of your emotional hurt that you will need medicines to combat the excess in stress hormones. Watch out if these symptoms lead you to have significant impairment in the different aspects in your life. If your family life, your office work, your relationships with your friends and colleagues become affected, it may be time to see the doctor.

Chapter 3: Why People Break Up

A burning question common for people during breakups is the question, "Why?". We want to understand how one person could break off with us after such a long time. We want to know what went wrong which led to the breakup. There is a great deal to understand because we want to understand why we are suffering right now. The answer must be satisfactory for us. If the answer is vague or we doubt the credibility of the answer, then there are more questions formed in our minds. The thought of 'why' occupies every waking moment, extending to our work hours, our personal lives, even preventing our sleep. The answer to this question would determine how we can accept the situation and the length of the hurting/healing process.

Through my own experiences, and hearing the breakup stories of other people, I have classified the common reasons why couples break up. I have classified reasons according to the "Predominantly my fault", "Predominantly your fault" and "Not our fault." These designations are only meant to create some order in the chaos of reasons. But they may not be mutually exclusive. For example, there are some reasons which can fall into both the "My fault" and "Not our fault" categories. Also, note that we don't have a category named "Our fault." This is not because there is no reason that involves both of you. In fact, there is no such category because all reasons are "Our fault" reasons. Remember that a relationship is never one-sided. Both sides are always affected and at fault at the result of a relationship. When a husband cheats on his wife, it is not purely his fault. The other person probably behaved in ways that also contribute to the breakup. Two people are needed to make a relationship work. And two people also are needed to make a relationship break apart. We put the designation 'predominantly' to say that there is more fault or weight on the person involved. We assume that it is both their fault, but one person may have the predominant reason for breaking.

Predominantly My Fault

These reasons refer to those that involve deficiencies that come from your own side. You have to be honest enough to admit that you are at fault when it comes to the relationship. Especially men who have big egos, admitting to a fault is tantamount to weakness. But the more we are able to accept that it is our fault predominantly, the more we are able to understand and move on from the relationship. The more we deny our involvement, the more confused we will be. We can be more defensive, leading to the cessation of communication. Not owning up to your mistakes may become a pattern and eventually, the breakup will repeat to the next relationships.

1. Lack of Time

Many couples break up because you have just lost time for each other. In your pursuit to give the good life for your partner, you may spend too much time in the office than attending to her needs. Excelling well in the workplace is not bad at all. In fact, it is a good sign of initiative and industriousness, a mark that you want to be a good provider in the family. But when you carry it to the extreme, your partner may feel left out. It is not enough that you provide well for your family. Your presence and your time are equally important. Giving your partner a house, a car, jewelry, flowers or money may be enough for you. But perhaps, all they wanted to have was you by their side, listening to them or simply sharing the time together. Later on, when you have a family, your children will also demand time from you. Children will also want you to be there during school activities, when they feel sad or afraid about school, when they are struggling with their sexuality or simply when they feel they need a father by their side. Time is very important in a relationship.

If you feel that you are not ready to give enough time to your partner, then admit that you are not ready for a relationship. Perhaps you should focus on your career first before entertaining anything else. In this way, you can do well in your work without the hassle of making somebody wait on you. Relationships are very time-consuming so be prepared when you enter one. What is good with today's advancing technology, you can actually reach out to your loved ones more readily. If you are living in a different place, you can simply call your partner and spend quality time talking. If you are in a different time zone, negotiate the best time you can call and update each other. Your partner may have left you because she does not feel loved enough when you don't give enough time especially when all the means are available to you.

2. Lack of Interest

Giving time is only part of the greater reason which is interest. A stronger word for this is love. Do you even love the person you are with? You may have been initially attracted to her. The attraction must have been intense that you decided to make it official and became real boyfriends and girlfriends. But later on, you may have gotten tired of her. Dinners with her may seem boring and predictable. If you were attracted to her pretty face at first, after some time, you get to see the pores on her face, how unappealing her breath is in the morning or how shrill her voice is. When you lose interest in a person, you may find the smallest details not to like them. And that shows even if you don't express it overtly.

Women are very intuitive about this. You may not say it directly to them, but they can feel if you are not anymore into them. If before you used to bring them flowers, they can feel the lack of interest when you don't bring flowers anymore. If you don't hold their hands, if you forget anniversaries, if you come up late during dates, if you don't call them when you get home, if you are not as loving anymore, they would know. It's an instinct they have developed from being with the person for a long time. You begin to see patterns of behavior and notice deviations from those patterns. Non-verbals actually speak more than uttered words. By your gestures and lack of attention to them, women are able to sense when they are not loved anymore. So check yourself. Do you really love this person or do you just want to stay for the sake of staying in a relationship? If this is not resolved, a lukewarm kind of relationship develops and sooner or later, dies a natural death by disinterest.

3. Lack of Communication

A common point of fights is the lack of communication. When couples stop talking altogether, there is a big problem that is not being resolved. If you have a lot of things you want to tell your partner but you don't want to for fear of being judged, of rocking the boat or hurting her feelings you are actually inflicting more pain by not telling anything. You may think that what you are feeling is petty and trivial. But if it is really important to you, those little things pile up in the long term and may simply explode when you least expect it. If you are feeling anything, tell your partner about it, regardless of how small or important it is. You have to think that the other person is your best friend, somebody who will understand you even if it is irrational or trivial. You are able to work out issues better when there is a clear communication system between you. Love in a relationship dies when couples keep secrets from each other.

Effective communication is built when couples know what and how to tell each other. The content must be clear and concise. Don't tell your partner that you don't like something about her just for no apparent reason. Be clear in what you want to say. But a greater part is not just in the content of the message but more importantly, how you say it. The timing of your feedback, the tone of your voice, the body language, the facial expression all contribute to packaging an effective message. Some men may think that women are mind readers and that simply by grunting, you can get your message across. Other men may mean well, but the way they say things may come across differently to women. Check yourself. Do you have a communication issue? Do you feel that you make yourself understood and that you can understand your partner? Do you think you have problems with your partner that you don't talk about? Check your communication skills because that may be the cause of your breakup.

4. Lack of Trust

It is flattering to be jealous. When you love a person too much, you can be very protective of her and would want to know how she is doing most of the time. When other men with dubious intentions are around her, you want to be there to protect your girl. The intention to show your love by being protective is understandable and even romantic. But too much of it can actually be stifling. Some men can be overly jealous bordering on obsessive behavior. They want to know exactly where their partner is, what she is doing, who she is with. They will immediately be alarmed if she failed to mention spontaneous meetings or come a few minutes late on a date. This leads to prolonged fights and the unearthing of past issues. Men are especially jealous of the girl's exes. They see them as active threats which may resurrect at any point that the girl is unprotected. Any text, post or picture associated with the girl's ex and the men go on an accusing spree. They may even result in threatening the other party verbally or physically, leading to embarrassing confrontations. They justify the jealousy by saying that they love the girl too much that is why they are protective.

Without a healthy sense of trust, the relationship cannot thrive. The girl will always feel that she is not trusted, while the guy will always feel that he will be betrayed. If the relationship is not built on trust, you will always find things to blame each other on. The girl will feel stifled and before long will lose interest with you. The things you blame on her might actually come true when she realizes that she would be better off with her exes. More than love, she will feel traumatized from your behavior. And for yourself, it is not healthy to have excessive jealousy. True love is when you are secure enough to let the other be free. Love means allowing space for the other to grow. This does not mean that you should stop worrying about her. It only means that you should love her in a way that will allow her to live her life fully. Ask yourself if you have been overly jealous. This might be the trigger for your breakup.

5. Lack of Financial Stability and Drive

One stereotype on men is that they should be good providers. They are usually the ones who work and put food on the table. Back in the old days, men were designated to this position because of their physique, allowing them to hunt and farm. Throughout the generations, they have been depended upon to shoulder the family income, provide the budget for everyday subsistence, ensure the education of children and allow for occasional luxuries. Today, we see a shift in perspective where women too can also be providers. Families may be set up with both parents working while extended families take care of the children. Women are venturing in traditionally male work, breaking glass ceilings and providing income to the family. In spite of these changes, the stereotype on men remains, with them expected to still be the main provider.

If your partner does not see you as a good provider, then the relationship may be compromised. It does not mean that you have to be rich. If that were the case, then only those in the upper economic bracket would have relationships. What is important for women is that they see their men trying and having a clear direction in terms of providing for their family. The type of work, the company you belong to, the position you hold are all very appealing because all of these factors show a high level of status. If you are not perceived as reaching that status or you are not seen as working towards that, your attractiveness as a partner diminishes. Gone are the days of love alone is enough. The capacity to provide is also a significant factor in choosing partners. When a girl sees that you are not trying your best to get a job, when you have poor financial management, when you are burdened with a lot of debt, the girl may leave you for better pastures. She might love you enough to give you a chance to prove yourself. But they are also concerned with the kind of life they will live with you. So, you have to show them that you can give them a good life, not necessarily a rich life. A drive to succeed is very attractive to women. And the opposite of that which is mediocrity or laziness is a death blow to any relationship.

6. A Third Party

This would be rather self-explanatory. A third party is one of the top reasons why couples break up. The involvement of the third party can be seen in a spectrum of intensity. The third party may be imagined, as when your girlfriend accuses you of having an affair but in reality, there is none. Another is when you simply flirted with the third party, either in conversation, in a date, through text or through social media. No sexual act has transpired, but there is an ongoing flirtation that your girlfriend caught and thus ended your relationship. Or the relationship with the third party could go in full swing, with singular or multiple sexual encounters. Some men may even entertain more than one affair, complete with a separate house or even children in tow. The breakup will only be in place once you get caught by your girlfriend.

What is the solution to this? The misogynistic answer is of course, not to get caught. Your relationship will prosper only as long as your girlfriend is ignorant of the double-dealings you engage in. But the more mature answer is, of course, to settle within yourself the cause of the affair. Were you simply tired of your current girlfriend? Is your relationship going too steady that you needed some excitement in your life? Are there needs you feel are not met and that you can find in someone else? Does having an affair excite you? Are there things you want to experience that is not possible with a monogamous relationship? It will be terribly unfair for you and for the girl if you keep on dating and still having a third party. The more mature move is really to assess how much you love the person and how committed and loyal you can be in spite of the ups and downs of life.

For some women, they may give second chances. The majority, of course, will breakup with you, especially if they caught you in the act or there are a lot of details that don't match up. You should be smart enough to accept that you cheated and that is the cause of your breakup. If given a second chance, well and good. But if you don't resolve your first issue on why you cheated, then the affairs might repeat itself. You would have to go through your own issues and sort these out before you can launch yourself in the relationship. If you feel that you are not ready to settle, then be very clear with that. Expect the consequences of cheating and resolve to be better.

7. Bad Habits, Vices and Destructive Behavior

This is a no-brainer, but you would be surprised how some men may not be aware of the negative effect of their bad habits, vices and destructive behavior. Perhaps they grew up in a world where people will accept them no matter what they do. But in the real world, what you do has an effect on other people. Nobody wants to be in a relationship where you get a lot of verbal abuse, physical injuries or traumatizing threats. Nobody wants to take care of a person with uncontrolled anger management issues where they will lash out at their partner when they feel provoked. Nobody wants to date someone who can get physically violent when drunk. Few would tolerate outright smoking cigarettes or weed inside a house with children. If your partner can tolerate you, then you are a match for each other. The greater majority of women would not stand up to this kind of abuse.

So, ask yourself, "Do I have bad habits, vices and destructive behavior?" You may be aware that you have some bad habits, but you don't feel that they have a negative effect on others. If you are in a relationship, part of loving is being able to change yourself to become a better person. You want to be your best self and hopefully the other can accept you for it. When you have anger management issues and you go on road rage when somebody cuts you, you are not being your best self. When you smoke weed in the house with children, you are not in your best self. When you need to abuse your partner when you are drunk physically, you are not in your best self. If your partner can tolerate this setup, then she is not in her best self either, and both of you should seek help. If you want to continue living this kind of life, then a relationship might not be for you. If you are willing to change, you should do so because you think that you want to be the best self you can be both for yourself and for your partner. The act of love changes people so they can be their best self. Expect the breakup if you are not willing to be in your best self.

Predominantly Your Fault

Having said all these seven commandments of "Predominantly My Fault", the next item is relatively easy. "Predominantly Your Fault" is every item on the previous list except that the locus of blame is on the other. The other party is also capable of lacking in time, interest, communication, trust and drive. Your girlfriend is also capable of cheating and exhibiting bad habits, vices and destructive behavior. These items are not exclusive to either sexes; they are common vulnerabilities we have as humans.

The name of the game then is where to put the blame predominantly on. Your assessment of the breakup may be different from how your girlfriend sees it. You may think that she has no time for you, but it may also be the case that you don't have time for her. You may think that she cheated on you, but for her, you cheated on her first. The blame game is on when couples fail to reach a level of understanding and honesty. The relationship breaks naturally when couples cannot admit to their mistakes and ask for forgiveness. If you keep on blaming her and not admitting to your own mistakes, then there is no way the relationship will continue. The converse is also true. As long as she is in denial of her shortcomings and does not seek forgiveness, then you should not expect to move further together. Instead of playing the blame game, healthy couples should play the "I am sorry and I forgive you" game. This involves admitting to your own mistakes and apologizing sincerely. It is normal to make mistakes, and we all commit that at some point in our lives. But we should always strive to own up and correct our mistakes, lest they repeat themselves or we continue hurting the other.

Not Our Fault

The last category of reasons why couples break is under the term "Not our fault." These reasons do not put the blame on anyone in the relationship, but rather on the circumstance that you both are in. This is especially difficult because nobody is at fault here but the relationship will not work because the context and environment are not supportive of the relationship. The solution to these is either to try again in a different context or try to date another person in the same context. The results may then be in your favor. But here are just some reasons why couples breakup with nobody to blame.

1. Parent's Disapproval

This is a classical trope seen throughout history, where the parents disapprove the relationship of the children. Romeo and Juliet epitomize this pattern of breakup but chose to go through extreme measures just to prove their point. The weight of the parent's decisions on their children's marriages differ across cultures. There are cultures that are more permissive, where children can actually choose their own partners. There are cultures that are very restrictive, even to the point of arranging the marriages even though their children are at a young age. And there are cultures that fit in between these extremities, allowing for some amount of independence on children but also enforcing some rules depending on the choice of partner. In Asian contexts for example, parents are highly regarded and their permission is sought first before the children can marry. When the parents disapprove, the children may obey their parents and seek other partners who are more suitable for them. Or in some cases, children may do their own, marrying the partner they love, but risk estrangement from the family.

Again, this is not a fault of either the guy or the girl in the relationship. They are simply born in families and cultures which are more communal in nature. Having parents decide for you is not necessarily bad in itself. There is a cultural value being upheld in this, where society believes that the experience of parents makes them better people to decide for their children. We cannot judge the cultural values of a particular people when it comes to marriage because there is a great historical tradition surrounding these values. We can only seek to understand why our parents are the way they are. As children, we are asked both to respect them and to state our own opinions on the matter. At the end of the day, you are the one marrying the other person and not your parents. But breakups will happen if the families do not feel a sense of peace regarding the relationship.

2. Difference in Priorities

For you, a career might be your top priority. For the girl, having children may be the top priority. When these priorities clash, a lot of misunderstandings happen and this can lead to a shaky relationship or even an eventual breakup. This item may also include the lack of interest and time reasons on the previous list. When couples have differing priorities, they are not able to give time to each other. The interest is diminished as they pursue their priorities. There is also a lack of communication as couples fail to reconcile the difference in priorities.

But having a different priority is not in itself bad. You should not feel guilty that you prioritize your career first before the relationship. If you feel that you should work first and climb up the corporate ladder while you still can and while the opportunity is there, then you should pursue your own goals. Do not also stop your partner from achieving her priorities. If she feels that she wants to improve herself more, to gain more skills in the workplace, to be promoted in her work, then let her become her best self. Just make sure that you understand where the other is and you can still accept each other. If you feel that the difference in priorities is not something you can accept, then it is understandable that you break up. There is no need to keep on blaming each other, because you are simply following your own dreams. If you want to blame it on anything, blame it on the situation. Perhaps in a different context, the relationship will work. But until then, it might be better off if you focus on your priorities.

3. Medical Conditions and Acts of God

Nobody wants to get sick or plans to procure a disease. However, much you can prepare for a disease such as good diet and exercise, tons of vitamins and vaccination, you can still get sick. Even the healthiest of people can develop a debilitating disease such as a stroke or cancer. Science may have a lot of answers but not all of them. You may be a manager at a prestigious firm, but you still can suddenly develop an aneurysm. Or you may be born with that condition and there is a limited number of things you can do about your situation. Nobody can ever really prepare and totally prevent diseases from happening.

You cannot also totally prevent acts of God from happening. You may be driving at a leisurely pace when a truck suddenly hits you and paralyzes you from the waist down. You may be vacationing somewhere in a beach and a hurricane develops, taking away your health and possessions. You may have stored your savings in the safest deposits and then a scammer may suddenly run off with your money. You may have served in the army because you love your country. But because of your ordeal, you contracted a post-traumatic stress disorder. These are acts of God we can never truly prevent and prepare for. Bad luck happens even to the best of people.

And this can have an effect on your relationship. When your partner cannot accept the situation you are flung in, you cannot blame them for breaking up with you. After being diagnosed with a stroke, your girlfriend may not be able to accept this and leave you for someone healthier. You may love your girlfriend very much, but when she starts exhibiting behaviors leading to a psychiatric disorder, you may feel unprepared for such a situation and break off the relationship. Leaving someone in their most vulnerable time is downright mean. But it happens and you cannot blame anyone, either her or especially yourself, for the situation. Bad luck just happens, and breakups may be due to bad luck.

Knowing these reasons may give you an idea why you broke up. There are a million other reasons out there for breakups but these are just the common ones. The point of going through each reason is for you to have some cognitive closure on what happened. Part of the healing is begun when you have understood the situation. There will be times when your reason for breaking up is never rational, or that the girl just simply left. This is the more painful kind of breakup because there is nothing to understand. With understanding comes the readiness to accept the situation, no matter how difficult it currently is. Without understanding, the breakup is more difficult to carry. For your peace of mind, try to understand what happened.

Chapter 4: Understanding Your Feelings

It is commonly held that men are raised not to show any feelings. When we were growing up, we were taught that crying is a sign of weakness, a loss of masculinity, a defect in our personality. When we are hurt, we are told to keep the pain and project a tough exterior, lest other people bully us for being a coward. And we carry this thinking throughout our lives. It is reinforced when we grow up as adolescents. People are bullied for being too sensitive or showing emotions. It is an achievement if bullies are able to make their prey cry in public, as though crying was a shameful act. We carry this in our relationships, where we feel the need to be strong in spite of the pain we feel inside. Men are expected to be invulnerable to hurt and keep on being strong no matter what happens.

This thinking, though highly prevalent and pervasive, a destructive kind of thinking that affects men and their relationships. This thinking disregards the truth that everyone has feelings. If you step on a nail, you feel pain. When somebody backstabs you, you feel betrayed. If a person cheats on you, you feel angry. When somebody gives you a present, you feel happy. We have forgotten how it is to feel because society has expected that we don't have feelings. But we have. When we don't express our feelings, they can get buried inside our consciousness, like a graveyard of feelings. But it doesn't mean that they are dead forever. Our repressed feelings can come back and express themselves at times when we least expect it. All your repressed feelings can come rushing in at a moment when you are very vulnerable. This is especially true when traumatic things like a breakup happen. You are filled with a lot of feelings you don't understand that you are capable of.

In order to begin the process of healing after a breakup, the very first thing you should do is to tune in to your true feelings. If your feelings are not expressed, they can be very destructive, to yourself and to others. Imagine a balloon that you fill up with a lot of air. The more air you fill it up, the more it will expand. But as more air comes in, the pressure builds up, to the point that it will explode and pop the balloon. Feelings work in the same way. The more that you repress them, the more they will build up inside of you. There is intense pressure as they are not able to go out. At a critical point, they will simply explode. This could be in the form of exhibiting violent behavior as a result of a breakup. You may start becoming addicted to drinking and drugs as a consequence of repressing your feelings. You may contemplate suicide or even threaten the girl because you cannot control your feelings anymore. Before you hurt yourself and others, you must begin to let some steam out. Let your feelings express themselves, in a controlled manner, before they explode. Allow yourself to feel all those things you have repressed for a long time. And you will feel lighter as a result of the process.

How do you even start tuning in to your feelings if you don't know what they are? Most people when asked the question, "How are you?" will reply "I am ok." Being ok is not a feeling. Being ok is the reply of a person who does not know his true feelings. We have been used to feel ok because we do not know what are true feelings are. The very first step is naming your feelings. When we are able to name our feeling, we can pinpoint exactly what we are experiencing. You cannot name and tune in to your feelings upon command. You need to give space and time where the feelings can express themselves. It might be good to spend some quiet moments in a day just to coax your feelings to reveal themselves. If you are too busy with socializing or with work, you will not be able to pay attention to your feelings and you will miss the opportunity to name them.

There are many kinds of feelings. But these can be summed up in four basic feelings. Other feelings are related to the four basic ones and are extensions of it. The four feelings are glad, mad, sad, and afraid. I have made the names catchier so you can remember them better. As we go through the different feelings, try to identify if this is the central feeling you are experiencing at this point.

1. Glad

We are all familiar with the feeling of happiness. When we eat ice cream, we feel happy. When we are rewarded with money, we feel happy. When we are given a promotion we longed for, we are happy. When we are doing the things we love, we are happy. Pleasure is a basic feeling of humans and we are programmed to feel happy.

In fact, science has isolated endorphins in our brain that are responsible for this happiness. When we feel happy, endorphins are released in our system and we interpret this as pleasure. And we seek ways to be happier as the body craves more of the endorphins.

Happiness also covers a broad spectrum of feelings. You can be mildly amused. You can feel comfortable and easy. You can feel amazed and ecstatic. The most extreme happiness is when you are delirious. The intensity of happiness depends on the situation and your own personality. It is good if you are able to sense how intense your happiness is in certain situations.

Is happiness possible immediately after a breakup? The usual answer is of course no. Breakups are very stressful situations and predispose you to negative feelings, least of all happiness. But, happiness is possible after a breakup. This is an important thing to remember. Your sadness or your anger will pass away and there will come a time when you will be happy again. It is not good to immediately jump to happiness just because you crave it now. Happiness comes at the right time and context. Don't force yourself to be happy, if you really are not. In time, you can be happy, so simply wait expectantly for it.

2. Mad

Anger is one of the core feelings we can experience when we encounter a breakup. We feel angry when there is a sense of betrayal. You feel angry when the reasons for the breakup are not satisfactory to you. You feel angry when the people you trusted have broken it, most especially your girlfriend. Physically, you can experience this as a rush of adrenaline in your blood as though you are primed to fight an enemy. You want to punch someone, to release that anger in some way before it consumes you.

Like happiness, anger has a spectrum of feelings associated with it. You can feel mildly irritated at a situation. You can feel annoyed at someone. You can feel mad and vengeful. The most extreme of this is furious, the type where you just want to swoop on someone and inflict damage. Recognize the different anger intensities and place your anger on the scale.

Three things are important in our understanding of anger. One, we have to recognize that it is possible that anger can be self-directed. In a breakup, we may feel that we are angry at ourselves for not being our best selves. We may blame ourselves for the situation. We are angry that we have been vulnerable. Recognize that we can be angry at ourselves. The second insight is that anger has to be expressed. What is good in humans is that we are capable of choosing the kind of expression appropriate for releasing anger. There is the usual punching of someone or banging of door or breaking of plates. There are extreme measures which involve heinous crimes as a result of blinding anger. We can choose to do this and suffer the consequences. But we are also free to choose non-destructive ways of releasing anger. Some ways include saying what you want to say out loud. You need to verbalize your anger so that it is released bit by bit. If you need to curse, curse away. If you need to shout, shout away. Don't keep it in, just let the anger burst and be free from it. Or you can use physical activities to release the anger. Some go for boxing or for contact sports to release the stress. Some run to get off the steam. Do what works for you. And last insight on anger involves time. Like all other feelings, anger passes away. You cannot remain angry for a very long time. You have to learn how to let it go when it is no longer needed. You cannot spend your whole life being angry at a particular person. Express it, release it and it will pass away.

3. Sad

This is the feeling most people have after a breakup. Most of the chapter on symptoms of a breakup pertain actually to sadness. We are sad because something we value is lost from us. We are sad because we have invested so much on a person only to be disappointed. It can affect our mood, our outlook on life, our appetite, our sleep, every activity we have. Sadness can be the only emotion we feel when we are traumatized.

It is important to recognize the spectrum of sadness because we have to note which the pathological ones are. Sadness can range from simple displeasure to dismay. It can develop into agony or hurt or anguish, extending to grief or sorrow or melancholy. These are normal expressions of sadness. What merits a thorough observation and at times medical intervention is when we feel depressed. This pertains to a pervasive sadness that we feel for a prolonged amount of time such as 6 months and significantly affects our functioning in daily life. When this is observed, it is warranted to seek medical help.

4. Afraid

The last feeling is fear. This is one of the most primal feelings associated with the flight response. Humans are afraid of many things from simple phobias like snakes, heights or open spaces. You can develop anxiety over situations where you cannot control everything. You can be afraid of the unknown. In a relationship, being afraid is very much possible. You are afraid of disappointing the people who expected your relationship to work out. You are afraid of facing a future without your girlfriend. You are afraid that you will never be loved again. And this fear can be very crippling. Trust issues develop as people are afraid to try again. Examine yourself if you feel afraid for yourself.

The biological response to fear is flight. In the ancient times, when Stone Age people encounter an animal they think they cannot defeat, they run from it. When armies size up a battalion they cannot defeat, they will retreat. When you look at a competition in sports, you feel affected and you might want to back out. The flight response accompanies fear. But the interesting thing about fear is that it can be imagined. There are real threats in the physical world. When a truck is rushing towards your car, you should feel afraid and get out. But there are imagined fears which we think are real. When you feel afraid that you won't be loved anymore, that is an imagined fear. You don't know the future so you feel anxious and claim defeat even though it has not transpired. Fear gives you the comfort of anticipating future events. Being afraid is easier than being courageous. Sometimes, imagined fear is more powerful than actual fear. Watch out for this lest you be fooled with projections of unreal fear.

Were you able to name your feelings? Naming is a difficult process because we are not used to listening to our feelings. We are comfortable in happiness, but we may feel that being sad or afraid is emasculating. We may have a dominant feeling, but it is possible to have different and simultaneous feelings. You feel angry but also sad and afraid. Recognize these different feelings, isolate them and see how they came about. When you are able to recognize and understand your feelings, you are one step closer to healing yourself after a breakup. Be gentle on yourself. Find a space where you can just be free to be your real self. Do not rush yourself and let the feelings wash over you.

Chapter 5: The Science of Getting Over a Breakup

At this point, we are now ready to come up with some means of providing you with bulletproof plans to get over a breakup. We strongly emphasize that you cannot jump to this chapter if you have not accomplished the exercise in the previous chapter. Feelings are very important in breakups and the only way you can be able to heal yourself is if you tune in and name your feelings. If you skip to this chapter, you are hiding from your own true feelings and the guidelines will only reinforce the hard shell you are protecting. Recognize that you are hurt because a breakup is always hurtful, no matter how you might cushion yourself from it. Being true to your feelings may be the most important step to get over any breakup.

The next items are a product of my own experience of healing and listening to the stories of how others were able to move on. I had made a lot of mistakes after my breakup but these next steps allowed me to bounce back and energized to live fully again. I also enjoyed hearing stories of healing from other people who were also heartbroken. Hopefully, these tips will also jumpstart your own journey to wellness.

Love Yourself

The first thing you should always remember is that you are good. The experience of breaking up is shattering and traumatizing. A lot of emotions and thoughts may be running through you, most of them gloomy or defeatist even. You will doubt yourself and your capabilities. Because of the breakup you will not like yourself, and even blame yourself for being weak and being a loser. Before you start on this masochistic spree, remember that you are good. Being good does not necessarily mean that you are talented, which undoubtedly you are. Being good does not refer to any skill, knowledge or trait that you have. Being good simply means that as a person, you are loving and are loveable. Never forget that. Do not listen to your ex when she tells you that you are worthless. She may not be right for you if she says that. Do not listen to yourself when you self-harm with doubts and insecurities. Remember that you are good, loving and capable of being loved.

The experience of brokenness is a good opportunity to look at those broken pieces of yourself once again. Before you can engage in another relationship, you must be able to put yourself back together first. You have to appreciate that all those jagged pieces of yourself are beautiful. You may be not as good-looking as other. But there is nothing wrong with that. You may have made a lot of mistakes like cheating or not finding time for your partner. Those are realities you have to accept as part of yourself. Gather these broken pieces of yours and recognize that you are beautiful in spite of all the cracks in your personality. In fact, these painful experiences are the ones that make you a stronger person.

There are many ways you can love yourself. On the physical aspect, learn to take care of yourself. There is nothing more satisfying than exacting revenge by looking good. Try out a new haircut. Treat yourself to a spa or to a massage. Work out and build those muscles again. Don't binge on bad food. Get enough sleep. Buy new clothes or purchase a sweet-smelling perfume. You can be sad, but you can still look awesome. Do not let the other person hurt you enough to make you look grubby or neglected. This is the only body you've got so you have to take care of it for the next person you will love.

You can also love yourself by taking a long break. Working immediately after a breakup may only produce bad output because you are still carrying that emotional weight to your desk. Take some time off like a few days so you can just be by yourself. Take a vacation so you don't feel stressed. Breakups may be the best reason for taking a break from the office. You need to recharge yourself so that you can continue becoming productive. Use the time to become intimate with your feelings, attending to them exclusively. The work will even improve if you take a break and find yourself.

Detox from Social Media

It is a good idea to simply cut off from social media. Apps like Facebook, Twitter, Instagram, etc. may be very toxic to a person who is undergoing a breakup. You need to stop stalking your ex online because you will simply reinforce the hurt each time you like her post or read her tweets. The less exposure to your ex, the faster you will be able to heal. When you are in social media, there is also a tendency to compare yourself with others. The posts of other people may show them having a good time, accomplishing a lot of things, being in places where you want to be. The tendency for someone hooked on social media is to compare your situation with what you are seeing. Instead of feeling better about yourself, you begin being jealous of other people taking a vacation. Instead of being able to move on, the posts of other couples doing sweet stuff together may only reinvigorate your hurt.

Life is possible without social media. You will be surprised that you can actually survive the day without glancing at your phone. This may be difficult at first because there is a natural instinct to check your pockets when you hear a vibration. But when you take away your devices far from reach, you will feel a load being lifted away from you. There is greater freedom felt when you realize that you need not be compelled to make a statement or to view the lives of others. By refraining from social media even for a short while, all the toxins of anxiety and comparison are sifted out from your system. You can return after a while, but you will see that there is a sustainable life outside of the social media prison we are currently in.

Rekindle Friendships

Use this opportunity to meet other people. Your world had become smaller when you focused only on one person. With your girlfriend, you may have cut off times from others because you were doing activities together. Now that you are apart, it may be time to revisit old friends and colleagues you may have missed. We emphasize here rekindling friendships, and not romances. This is to point that not all relationships need to be romantic. When we relate to other people, we don't need to own them or date them exclusively.

We have to recognize that we can be friends with other people without entering into romantic relationships with them.

Your friends will also serve as your support system. It is at your most vulnerable moments that you need to surround yourself with friends. Men are not used to this because they want to project a tough image that does not need help from anyone. But in reality, they are in a lot of pain and may need some help. By rekindling friendships, you are opening yourself to others and to their help. Just by sharing stories with them, you may feel some sense of healing at being able to relate to other people once again. You can seek advice from your friends. They may help you recover from your past relationships by bringing back old memories of better times. The sense of being with other people who will not judge you is a fool-proof plan to get over anybody.

Discover Passions

Instead of isolating yourself in the room, take the opportunity to discover hobbies you may have forgotten. The tendency for us after a breakup is just to stay in our rooms, binge on unhealthy food, turn on the telly and drink our sorrows away. This may be our initial coping mechanism but staying in that dark routine will only push you to further depression. Instead of moping away, use the time to take that old camera you used to click away, unearth the brushes you used to paint with or tinker with old toys you kept way back. Instead of focusing on your problems, you need to divert your attention to other stimuli. The world does not revolve around your girlfriend and rediscovering passions are a good way to expand your world.

You can also try to do new things. If you have never tried skydiving before, now is a good opportunity. If you've dreamt of scuba diving but didn't have the courage before, now is the best time to try. If cooking has always fascinated you, try enrolling in a class right now. When you do new things, you are stimulating other parts of your brain. Instead of focusing on your pain, you are able to redirect that sorrow to some productive. The love you fill inside is just overflowing and it will need a way to be expressed. A good option is to channel that into new hobbies and passions.

Develop New Routines

Instead of walking to your office in your usual route, try a different one. If you always used a taxi to go back home, try using the bus. If you always drank the same coffee, try a different flavor. When you do new things, you are unlocking your mind from the usual. There is a sense of creation, as the brain tries to figure in the new images and experiences. If you want to forget the old routines, then make new ones. If you always associate that park bench with your girlfriend, ditch that route so you can meet other people. The goal is not to forget your ex. The goal is to develop new experiences so you can expand your world.

New routines may also be applied in the office. Use the opportunity to tackle new problems in the workplace. You can even solve old problems using new techniques. Instead of the usual sales pitch, you can try an online advertisement just to shake the routine of the office. You become productive when you are trying something new. Before long, you won't even remember that you broke up with somebody.

Choose to Help

Odd as it may seem but helping others will facilitate the healing process for you. You are not actually empty when somebody breaks up with you. If you really loved that person, there is just a lot of love generated from each other. When that person leaves you, they don't necessarily take that love with them. There is just a lot of extra love inside you that needs to be channeled. You can make good use of that love and energy in an altruistic way.

Try helping out at an orphanage or visiting retirement homes. Volunteer in some cause or advocacy. Adopt a pet or engage in pet rescues. Babysit a cousin or visit a sick friend. These acts of kindness transform your hurt into something life-giving. In the process of giving yourself, you are actually rebuilding yourself. When you help other people, you begin to realize that they are broken too. You will see that they are in greater need of help than you. Some people have experienced worse things than we have. And there is no better person to help hurt people than hurt people also. Through your own brokenness, you see how they are also broken. By helping, you gather your and their broken pieces together in an attempt to make all of you whole. When you help, you are healing yourself and others in the process.

Forgive the Other

This may be the last thing on your mind. This person who has hurt you so much and inflicted you with pain you cannot recover from. Your ex has been unfair, a cheater, a nagger, a selfish person only concerned with their well-being. Exhaust your anger on that person. But one thing that will set you free from them is if you become the better person in spite of their mistakes. When you forgive, you are not choosing to forget the hurt they have inflicted on you. When you forgive your ex, you realize that the love you shared is more important than any hurt you have given each other. When you gift your ex with forgiveness, you are telling them that you love them enough to look over their petty mistakes. This does not mean that you get back together. Forgiveness also means remembering your mistakes so that you will not do it again to them or to other people.

But do not rush to forgive. Healing will take time and forgiveness is not instant. You will still feel pain whenever you see them. The old hurts may reopen. But when you remember how you love that person, you will realize that that love outweighs the hurt. With forgiveness, comes healing for you and for the other person. When you forgive, you also set the other person free.

Wait

The most difficult realization in breaking up is that everything will take time. Your feelings cannot be rushed. Your reactions and pain will not die down instantly. Your capacity to forgive does not become full overnight. There is a process to healing, and that can take time, from weeks to months or years. Each person will experience moving on differently from one another, some faster than others. Don't compare your process. You have a different context and that you should respect your body and emotions. Waiting is difficult because we are used to a world that is preoccupied with speed and instants. But the reality is that only time heals.

As you focus your attention on other things like your friends, your families, your work, new passions, new routines, new acquaintances, the waiting becomes bearable. Before you know it, a month or a year has passed. When you detox from social media, you will be surprised that the time has just passed by so fast. The waiting is actually tolerable when you begin loving other people once again. This does not mean exclusively romantic relationships. Waiting is strengthened when you express your love differently to many kinds of people. You become less bitter of your situation and you attract a lot of positivity by being positive yourself. Before you know it, you are over her. And should you meet her, you will

know that you have moved on when you can be
mature enough to be kind to each other.

Conclusion

Breaking up is one of the most traumatic things that can happen to people. Men would rather take this more heavily because they are not used to being left. When you break up, you question yourself, your talents and skills, your ability to love and to be loved. There is nothing more painful than breaking up with somebody you love. You will always remember her and the times you spend together, each recalling opening up the hurt anew. The heart gets broken not just once, but in every moment you remember her and the hurt she has caused you.

Hopefully, this book has equipped you with a lot of advice on how to move on from a breakup. If you were sensitive enough to notice, I have structured the book to include all the aspects of healing. In order to be healed from a breakup, there must be a cognitive resolution. Your mind must be able to understand what exactly happened, who was at fault and what could you have done to prevent the breakup from happening. Healing also happens when your emotions are addressed. You need to be able to name your feeling and listen to your body as it expresses these repressed feelings. Do not be embarrassed to feel gladness, sadness, madness and fear when you undergo these trying times. Feelings will come and go, so simply let it flow through you. And finally, healing is a result of changing your behavior and outlook on life. By forming new routines and meeting old friends, you begin to expand your world from the small one you used to nurture with your ex.

How should you relate to your ex after this? Is there a chance you can be friends with her? Should you win her over? Should you find another person? Only you can answer that. The future of your relationship is very much dependent on how you reacted to the situation, the status of your healing process, and your readiness to encounter her once more. It is not impossible to be friends with your ex. But everything will take time. It is possible that you may pursue her again. But this is not the immediate concern. You must first put yourself back together before you can win her over. It is definitely possible for you to meet other people and be in love once again. If you have a lot of love, you will always attract people who will love you back. But all of these scenarios are up for you to discover.

I have learned these the hard way. I went through the darkest times of my life without nobody to turn to. But through a lot of experimenting and listening to other people, I began to move out of the darkness I chose for myself. I realize that the night also passes and that we choose to become victims when we choose to be in the dark. There is an entire world out there and I chose to live. I hope this book has guided you from that path of darkness towards the light. There is no other way but through the night into the dawn. The journey becomes less difficult if you realize that you have someone with you. Take this book and see you on the lighter side.

Leave a Review

As an independent author with a small marketing budget, reviews are my livelihood on this platform. If you enjoyed this book, I'd really appreciate your honest feedback. I love hearing from my readers and I personally read every single review.

www.ingramcontent.com/pod-product-compliance
Lightning Source LLC
Chambersburg PA
CBHW051212250726
48655CB00006B/2363